Who Was
Sitting Bull?

Who Was
Sitting Bull?

by Stephanie Spinner

illustrated by Jim Eldridge

Penguin Workshop

To my sister, Wendy—SS

PENGUIN WORKSHOP
An Imprint of Penguin Random House LLC, New York

Visit us online at www.penguinrandomhouse.com.

Library of Congress Control Number: 2014958193

ISBN 9780448479651   20 19 18 17 16

Contents

Who Was
Sitting Bull?

When Sitting Bull was ten years old, he went on his first buffalo hunt. He was the only boy in a group of skilled warriors. He had made his bow and arrows himself and used them on birds, rabbits, and other small game. But he had never hunted buffalo.

Buffalo provided food and clothing for the tribe
Their hides were made into tepees. They were more
valuable to the Lakota Sioux than any other anima

And they were huge—sometimes two thousand pounds. When the hunters started to chase the herd, causing a stampede, Sitting Bull watched carefully. Then he found a young buffalo, raced after it on his pony, and brought it down with two shots from his bow.

When the hunters returned home and divided up their kill, Sitting Bull gave his buffalo to a family that had very little to eat. He did the same thing on his next hunt and on many more after that. The Lakota prized generosity, but it was unusual in such a young boy.

Sitting Bull grew up to be a great chief. He led many American Indian tribes in the long, hard fight to keep their land and their ways of life. Generous to the last, he gave everything he had to help his people.

Chapter 1
Slow

Sitting Bull was named Jumping Badger
when he was born in the spring of 1831, in South
Dakota. His father, a chief of the Hunkpapa
Sioux, was very happy to have a son in the family.

Jumping Badger proved to be an unusual child—very quiet and very watchful.

When he was a toddler, Jumping Badger never grabbed at anything he was offered, even food. Instead, he would look it over intently before taking it. When he was asked a question, he thought carefully about the answer. Because he never did anything quickly, his mother and two sisters stopped calling him Jumping Badger. They called him Slow instead.

Slow learned to ride a pony when he was three or four. A year or two later, his father gave him his first bow and arrow. They were small, but they worked, and Slow was soon using them to hunt rabbits, squirrels, and birds.

Before long, he made his own weapons.

Like other young boys in the tribe, Slow looked forward to hunting buffalo. The huge, lumbering creatures were all-important to the Hunkpapa, who ate buffalo meat and used buffalo hides for tepees, blankets, and clothing. They made spoons and cups out of buffalo horns, strung their bows with buffalo tendons, and made war paint with buffalo fat and colored powder. The buffalo gave them almost everything they needed, and for this, they were grateful. They prayed to a buffalo god and used a buffalo skull in religious ceremonies.

And they considered a boy's first buffalo hunt to be very important. It was his first step to manhood.

When Slow went on his first buffalo hunt, there were a dozen warriors in the hunting party, including his father and two uncles. Slow wanted to make them proud.

The hunters rode across the plains until they found a herd. Then they began to chase it. Hundreds of buffalo stampeded, raising thick, blinding clouds of dust. The earth shook.

The noise of the animals was deafening. Slow calmly found a young buffalo in the herd, chased it, and killed it with two shots from his bow.

Back at camp, he gave the meat to a family that needed food. The boy's kind deed made his father proud. Generosity was one of four qualities the Sioux admired most. The others were strength, wisdom, and bravery.

THE GREAT SIOUX NATION

IN THE 1830S, THE SIOUX, CALLED THE GREAT SIOUX NATION, WERE THE MOST POWERFUL AMERICAN INDIANS ON THE GREAT PLAINS. THEIR TERRITORY WAS VAST, ABOUT HALF A MILLION SQUARE MILES THAT STRETCHED FROM THE MISSOURI RIVER IN THE EAST TO THE YELLOWSTONE RIVER IN THE WEST, AND SOUTH FROM THE NORTH PLATTE RIVER ALL THE WAY UP TO CANADA. THE SIOUX TRAVELED OVER THEIR LAND FOR MOST OF THE YEAR, FOLLOWING HERDS OF BUFFALO.

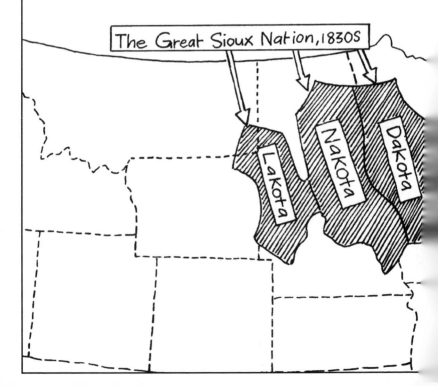

The Great Sioux Nation, 1830S

Lakota

Nakota

Dakota

THE SIOUX NATION WAS MADE UP OF THREE MAIN GROUPS: THE LAKOTA, THE DAKOTA, AND THE NAKOTA. THEY SPOKE THE SAME LANGUAGE (WITH SMALL DIFFERENCES) AND WORSHIPPED THE SAME "GREAT SPIRIT" CALLED WAKAN TANKA. EACH GROUP INCLUDED SEVERAL BRANCHES, OR TRIBES.

SITTING BULL'S FAMILY BELONGED TO ONE OF THE SEVEN LAKOTA TRIBES, THE HUNKPAPA. THE OTHER LAKOTA WERE THE BLACKFEET, THE BRULÉ, THE MINICONJOU, THE OGLALA, THE SANS ARC, AND THE TWO KETTLES.

THE TRIBES OF THE GREAT SIOUX NATION WERE FRIENDLY TO ONE ANOTHER. THEY LIVED APART, BUT WOULD SOMETIMES BAND TOGETHER TO HUNT. WHEN IT WAS NECESSARY, THEY FOUGHT TOGETHER AGAINST A COMMON ENEMY.

Chapter 2
Sitting Bull

Young Sioux boys spent a lot of time playing. They held footraces and pony races. They had shooting contests with their bows and arrows. They played tag and wrestled. They ambushed one another. Their games were a lot of fun, but they had a serious purpose, too. They were training—for the hunt and for war.

The Sioux waged war often.
They fought their enemies, the Crow
and the Assiniboin, every chance they got.

This meant killing enemy warriors, stealing their horses and weapons, and looting their camps. To the Sioux, fighting was a way to win honor and glory. One favorite saying was, "It is better to die on the battlefield than to grow old." For a Sioux man, the best way to die was to die fighting.

At fourteen, Slow was more than ready to join a war party. One of his uncles had died while fighting a band of Crow a few months before. Now, twenty warriors, including Slow's father, were getting ready to strike back. Slow watched

them while they painted themselves and their horses, gathered up their tomahawks, lances, and bows, and rode out of camp.

As the last of the men left, Slow made up his mind He covered his body with yellow paint.

He painted his horse red. Then he set out to join the war party.

They were on a hill, waiting. Below them, a band of Crow was riding across the plains. When Slow appeared, the men were silent. Then his father handed Slow a brightly painted stick called a *coup stick* (say: koo stick). "You have a fast horse," he said. "Do something brave."

Among the Sioux, hitting an enemy with a coup stick and then throwing him off his horse was the bravest thing a warrior could do. It was much harder than shooting a foe from a distance. So whoever did it first was considered the best fighter in the war party. Competition for first coup was intense.

The warrior who had planned the raid was supposed to give the signal to start the attack. But Slow couldn't wait. Coup stick in hand, he wheeled toward the Crow. The rest of the party followed. Seeing so many enemies, some of the Crow fled.

The braver ones stood their ground. Slow targeted one of them.

Galloping at great speed, he struck the Crow with the coup stick, knocked him down, and raced away, crying, "I, Slow, have conquered him!"

Then the rest of the party attacked, and the real fighting began. After killing all but a few of the Crow, and taking many of their horses, they rode back to camp in triumph.

Slow's father could hardly contain his pride. His son, a daring buffalo hunter from the age of ten, had now shown he was a bold warrior.

He deserved praise and the choicest buffalo meat at the feast! Slow got plenty of both. He was given a big, fast horse and two of his father's weapons—a beautiful  war shield and an eight-foot-long spear. To show that he had counted first coup, he was given a white eagle feather to wear in his hair. But Slow's greatest prize of all was a new name.

ONE PERSON, MANY NAMES

WHEN A CHILD WAS BORN INTO THE SIOUX NATION, HE OR SHE WAS GIVEN A BIRTH NAME THAT USUALLY LASTED THROUGH CHILDHOOD. SITTING BULL'S MOTHER WAS FIRST NAMED **MIXED DAY,** AND HIS FATHER WAS NAMED **RETURNS AGAIN.** LATER, THEIR NAMES CHANGED TO MARK IMPORTANT EVENTS. WHEN **MIXED DAY** GAVE BIRTH TO HER SON, SHE BECAME **HER HOLY DOOR.** WHEN A SACRED BUFFALO SPOKE TO HIM IN A VISION, **RETURNS AGAIN** TOOK THE NAME **SITTING BULL.**

LATER, WHEN SITTING BULL'S FATHER GAVE HIS NAME TO HIS SON, HE TOOK THE NAME **JUMPING BULL,** WHICH HE KEPT FOR THE REST OF HIS LIFE.

Toward the end of the feast, his father told everyone that Slow's bravery had earned him a new name. The chief had decided to give Slow *his* name—one that stood for strength, courage, and determination.

On that day, Slow became Sitting Bull.

When he was fourteen or fifteen, Sitting Bull went on a vision quest. This was something all Sioux boys did before they were considered men. With the help of a shaman, or holy man, the boy cleansed himself in a special tepee called a *sweat lodge*.

Then he went into the wilderness, where he smoked a sacred pipe, chanted, and prayed. He hoped for a glimpse of his future. At best, he would gain some  understanding of Wakan Tanka, the Great Spirit who ruled the world.

At the end of his vision quest, Sitting Bull told the shaman that he had seen Wakan Tanka. The Great Spirit came to him in a vision, as a bright light in the clouds. When they heard this, the tribal elders believed it was a sign that Sitting Bull would be a chief one day.

Sitting Bull got another sign about his future a few years later. It came in a dream.

Alone in the forest after hours of hunting, he lay down to rest and fell asleep. Almost immediately, he dreamed that he was running from a grizzly bear

It was gaining fast. His only weapons were a bow and arrow. They weren't the best defense against such a big animal. But he had no choice. With his heart racing, he turned and took aim.

Sitting Bull woke to hear a yellow woodpecker chattering from a high branch. He'd been dreaming, he realized. That was a relief!

And then the bird's chatter turned into words.

Lie still! it said. *Lie still!* Astonished, Sitting Bull obeyed. A moment later, a huge grizzly bear, just like the one in his dream, came out of the forest.

Approaching Sitting Bull, it leaned over him.
Sitting Bull lay there, wondering if these
moments would be his last—until the bear
grunted and ambled away.

Sitting Bull was so grateful for the bird's warning that he made up a song of thanks:

Pretty bird, you saw me and took pity on me;
You wish me to survive among the people.
O Bird People, from this day always
you shall be my relatives!

Now Sitting Bull knew that, like his father Jumping Bull, he could understand the language of birds and animals. People with this gift were called *wichasha wakan.* Their dreams and visions were said to predict the future. And like Jumping Bull, they were often tribal leaders.

Had the woodpecker saved Sitting Bull's life so he, too, could lead his people? He began to think so.

Chapter 3
War Chief

Sitting Bull was an outstanding warrior, always one of the first to strike, and the last to leave a battle. In 1851, at the age of twenty, the tribe's Strong Heart Society invited him to join. This was an honor, because Strong Hearts were famous for their courage.

The two bravest Strong Hearts each wore a red sash. When fighting, they would tie the sash to a lance—a long spear—and plant it in the ground. It was a sign that they would rather die than retreat.

COUP STICKS, EAGLE FEATHERS, SCALPS, AND WAR PAINT

A COUP STICK WAS MADE OF BRIGHTLY PAINTED WOOD OR BONE. IT WAS USUALLY ABOUT TWO FEET LONG AND OFTEN TRAILED AN EAGLE FEATHER. FIGHTERS COUNTING COUP WOULD CUT A NOTCH ON THE STICK FOR EVERY STRIKE THEY MADE.

A WARRIOR WHO WON FIRST COUP HAD THE RIGHT TO WEAR A WHITE EAGLE FEATHER. A WARRIOR WHO WAS WOUNDED IN BATTLE COULD WEAR A RED FEATHER. A WARRIOR WHO HAD COUNTED COUP MANY TIMES COULD WEAR A LONG EAGLE-FEATHER BONNET DECORATED WITH BEADS AND FUR TAILS. STRONG HEART LEADERS WORE A RED SASH AND A FEATHER HELMET WITH BUFFALO HORNS.

THE SIOUX BELIEVED THAT A PERSON'S HAIR WAS PART OF HIS OR HER SPIRIT, SO TAKING AN ENEMY'S SCALP MEANT TAKING AWAY ALL THAT PERSON'S POWER. WARRIORS DISPLAYED SCALPS ON THEIR LANCES OR HUNG THEM FROM THEIR HORSES' NECKS.

BEFORE GOING INTO BATTLE, WARRIORS PAINTED THEIR FACES AND BODIES WHITE, YELLOW, RED, AND BLUE. THEY PAINTED THEIR HORSES, TOO, WITH SYMBOLS LIKE ARROWS, HANDPRINTS, AND LIGHTNING BOLTS.

Not long after he joined the Strong Hearts, Sitting Bull performed his first Sun Dance. Held in early summer, the Sun Dance was an important ceremony for the Sioux. Those who took part did so for the good of the tribe. Any visions they had while dancing were thought to predict the future.

On the day of his first Sun Dance, Sitting Bull sat on the ground inside a big circle. His hands and feet were painted red, and his shoulders were painted blue. The shaman made cuts in Sitting Bull's chest and back, and inserted narrow wooden pegs into the cuts. The pegs were attached to rawhide strips hanging from a pole at the center of the circle. At the base of the pole was a sacred buffalo skull.

Sitting Bull went to the edge of the circle and began to dance. Staring at the sun, he sang prayers to Wakan Tanka for the safety and well-being of the Hunkpapa. He ignored his pain, dancing all day and into the night, until he finally collapsed from exhaustion.

In 1851 Sitting Bull married a young Hunkpapa woman called Light Hair. Unfortunately, she died in childbirth, and their little son died of illness when he was four. Not long after, Sitting Bull adopted his four-year-old nephew, One Bull. Because he had lost a son, and his sister Good Feather had two sons, the adoption made perfect sense to the tribe. As the Lakota liked to say, "we are all related."

Meanwhile, the Strong Hearts—the fiercest fighters on the Great Plains—chose Sitting Bull as their war chief. Though he was young to be a chief, he was already known for his strength, bravery, generosity, and wisdom.

In the years to come, he would need them all.

Chapter 4
Leader of the Sioux Nation

In the 1840s, many Lakota bartered for goods at the Fort Pierre trading post on the Missouri River. Otherwise, they had little to do with *wasichu*. That was their name for white people.

That changed in 1850, a year when fifty thousand *wasichu* came west. After the discovery of gold in 1848, many thousands had hurried through Sioux lands on their journey west to strike it rich. But these *wasichu* weren't miners. They were settlers, intending to stay.

In 1851, US government agents convinced many Plains tribes to sign an agreement called the Treaty of Fort Laramie. In exchange for allowing *wasichu* to travel safely across their territory, the tribes would get food and supplies. Most important, the tribes would keep control of their territory, as they always had. Representatives of the Arapaho, Assiniboin, Cheyenne, Crow, Shoshone, and Oglala and Brulé Sioux signed the treaty;

the Hunkpapa did not. US officials, who ignored the differences among the tribes, assumed that because the Oglala and Brulé signed the treaty, the Hunkpapa agreed to it, too. They were all Sioux, weren't they?

It was a serious misunderstanding—the first of many.

The Oregon Trail

After Fort Laramie, the settlers kept coming.
They usually traveled on the Oregon Trail,
which passed through present-day Nebraska.
With them came the cavalry—US Army soldiers
on horseback—for protection. The "bluecoats,"

as the Indians called them, built forts along
the routes and stocked them with cannons,
six-shooters, and long-range rifles. These weapons
were faster and more powerful than anything the
tribes had.

Frontier Fort

Army officers had little real authority over the tribes. Yet when they issued orders, they expected to be obeyed. As more and more soldiers came west, the tribes retreated to government-run reservations. In return for food and supplies, they gave up much of their land. Because the *wasichu* were not traveling through Hunkpapa territory in the late 1850s, Sitting Bull's people still lived undisturbed and hunted freely.

Then the Homestead Act of 1862 was passed. The US government promised 160 acres of Great Plains land to anyone who agreed to farm it for five years. Thousands of white settlers welcomed the opportunity. As their wagon trains came west,

more forts sprang up, bringing more bluecoats and
more weaponry. That same year, the government
approved the building of a new railroad. It would be
an engineering wonder, connecting the East Coast
with the West Coast across thousands of miles. It
would also cut right through Indian territory.

Sitting Bull had refused to sign the Fort Laramie Treaty of 1851. Now, eleven years later, tribes who had signed it were being forced off their land. The Santee Sioux, Arapaho, Cheyenne, Kiowa, and Pawnee, who lived to the east and south (in what is now Kansas, Nebraska, Iowa,

and Minnesota), were steadily losing their hunting and camping grounds. In fact, the *wasichu* were acting as if the Fort Laramie Treaty didn't exist. Sitting Bull decided they couldn't be trusted.

In July 1862, ten Hunkpapa chiefs sent a message to the Fort Berthold trading post.

It was on the Missouri River, in what is now North Dakota. The message said, "We wish you to stop the whites from traveling through our country, and if you do not stop them, we will."

The message was ignored. A month later, the Santee Sioux in Minnesota sent their own message, a much harsher one. After the tribe moved onto the reservation, their food rations had stopped. By August, they were starving. When they complained to the government agent in charge, he told them to eat grass.

Enraged, the Santee killed at least six hundred white settlers, innocent people who happened to be within striking range.

Hundreds of Santee warriors were quickly captured, tried, and found guilty. Thirty-eight were hanged for murder. It was a grim public execution, the largest in US history.

Some soldiers felt the rebel Indians had not been punished enough. General Henry Hastings Sibley and General Alfred Sully chased the fleeing Santee west with their troops. They killed many peaceful Indians along the way, more than once refusing to honor a white flag of surrender.

When they finally reached Dakota Territory, they were met with fierce resistance. Sitting Bull fought Sibley and Sully twice in the summer of 1863. In 1864, he led a huge war party, drawn from all the tribes of the Great Sioux Nation, against Sully. But even with 1,400 warriors, the Battle of Killdeer Mountain in North Dakota was a terrible defeat for the Sioux. Sully had 2,200 troops and twelve cannons. He forced the Sioux into the hills and then destroyed their village.

Another battle, this time in the badlands of North Dakota, also ended in defeat for the Sioux.

Sitting Bull knew that his people were great fighters. So did the bluecoats. One US general called them "good shots, good riders, and the best fighters the sun ever shone on." Another said, "They were then the best cavalry in the world; their like will never be seen again." But the bluecoats had more men and much better weapons. They would almost always have the advantage. Even so, Sitting Bull was determined to drive them away.

When the Civil War ended in June 1865, thousands of soldiers were shipped west. They built Fort Buford deep in Hunkpapa territory that year, again ignoring the Fort Laramie Treaty. Sitting Bull led raid after raid against Fort Buford. He also attacked settlers as far as two hundred miles away.

Meanwhile, the great Oglala Sioux chief Red Cloud was leading raids against settlers and soldiers on the Bozeman Trail, farther south. The trail led from the Missouri River to a cluster of gold mines in Montana. It passed right through Red Cloud's hunting grounds. When the government

RED CLOUD

built three forts along the trail, Red Cloud and his warriors attacked them relentlessly. The Hunkpapa and Cheyenne joined in the fight. After three years of trying to fight off the tribes, the US government called for a peace council, again at Fort Laramie.

Although Sitting Bull did not, many other Sioux chiefs attended. Hoping that peace with the whites was possible, they accepted the terms of the new treaty. They would give up their lands and move to the Great Sioux Reservation, a large area in the Dakota Territory (now South Dakota) that would be theirs forever. They would keep their hunting grounds, west of the reservation, for as long as the buffalo roamed. Their sacred Black Hills would be strictly off-limits to settlers.

In addition, the government would give them food, clothing, and money, and close the forts on the Bozeman Trail. By 1869, about seventeen thousand Sioux had moved to the reservation. Before joining them, Red Cloud and his warriors burned all three forts to the ground.

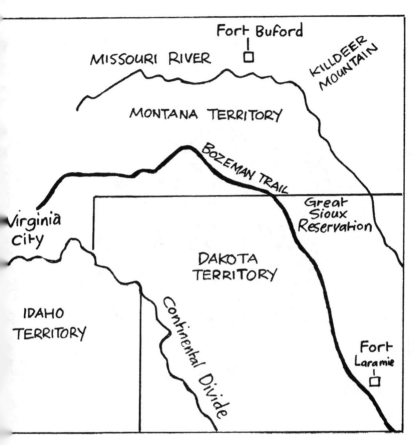

Sitting Bull had no respect for Indians who gave in to the government. "You are fools to make yourselves slaves to a piece of fat bacon, some hardtack, and a little sugar and coffee," he said.

He and the other nontreaty chiefs led their people west to the Wyoming Territory and set up camp near the Powder, Tongue, and Yellowstone Rivers. There were about three thousand Cheyenne,

Arapaho, Lakota, Dakota, and Nakota Sioux in the camp. Sitting Bull's uncle, Four Horns, a respected chief himself, felt they needed a strong leader. He proposed Sitting Bull, and the others agreed.

That summer, they held a huge ceremony
in his honor. He was presented with a lance, a
warbonnet of eagle feathers and ermine, and a
splendid white horse.

"When you tell us to fight, we shall fight,"
Four Horns promised Sitting Bull. "When you tell
us to make peace, we shall make peace."

Chapter 5
Gold

Sitting Bull must have known that he and his people faced many troubles. Their refusal to live on a reservation kept them free, but freedom came at a very high price. The buffalo herds, their main source of food, were disappearing.

After the cross-country railroad was completed in 1869, travelers took to shooting and killing buffalo right from the trains.

Men called *buffalo skinners*, armed with long-range rifles, killed buffalo by the thousands. They took their hides and left the carcasses to rot on the plains. They didn't care how much the Indians needed them. As they wiped out the herds, more and more Indians went hungry.

This was fine with many people. To them, the Indians were a threat to settlers and prevented progress. In their opinion, the entire United States belonged to the white people.

Sitting Bull often said he had no quarrel with the *wasichu* as long as they stayed away. But they were coming closer all the time. In 1872, US soldiers and a group of surveyors appeared in the Sioux hunting grounds near the Yellowstone River in Montana.

They spent days measuring land for another train line. To Sitting Bull, it was proof that the government had no intention of following the Treaty of 1868. He and the Oglala war chief Crazy Horse led several attacks against the soldiers, who retreated in 1873. For a while, Sioux hunting grounds were undisturbed.

Unfortunately, this wasn't true of the Black Hills. The Sioux thought of the Black Hills as the center of their world. It was a sacred place where

warriors had visions, and hunters always found game.

The Black Hills were also said to be rich with gold. In 1874, President Ulysses S. Grant sent soldiers, led by Lt. Col. George Armstrong Custer, to find out if the rumors were true.

ULYSSES S. GRANT

After several weeks, Custer reported that there *was* gold in the Black Hills. And there was a lot of it. Word spread quickly, and the sacred territory of the Sioux was soon overrun by miners.

The gold rush of 1874 angered the Sioux and worried President Grant. Government treaties had banned *wasichu* from the Black Hills. Grant sent in the US Army to uphold the law and to escort the miners out. The miners knew the soldiers wouldn't hurt them, and so they stayed.

Grant's next solution was to try to buy the Black Hills from the Sioux. Sitting Bull wasn't interested. "We want no white men here," he said. "The Black Hills belong to me. If the whites try to take them, I will fight." He persuaded many other chiefs not to sell the territory, either.

Because Sitting Bull blocked the sale of the Black Hills, he soon had powerful enemies in Washington, DC. Everyone in the government's Office of Indian Affairs considered him a troublemaker. They convinced Grant that if he wanted the Black Hills (and he did), he would have to use force.

As a result, the government announced a new policy toward the nontreaty Indians. In December 1875, agents in Sioux territory were told that any Indian who did not move to the Great Sioux Reservation by January 31, 1876, would be considered a *hostile*. Hostiles could be arrested, and even shot on sight.

Heavy snows and harsh winter cold on the Great Plains that month made travel almost impossible. The mail was slow, and most Indians didn't hear about the new policy until the very end of the year. They couldn't move, even if they'd wanted to. They were camped for the winter and would stay there until spring.

If officials in Washington, DC, had considered the weather on the plains, they might have waited until spring to issue their orders. They might have set a deadline the Indians could meet. But their goal wasn't to avoid conflict with the Indians. In fact, it was the opposite. As they saw it, the only way to take the Black Hills was by forcing the Indians into war.

By the time the nontreaty Indians heard what the government wanted, they had missed the deadline for moving and were already "hostiles." The Great Sioux War of 1876 had begun.

The cold and snow held off the US Army until March. Then General George Crook sent troops to attack a camp of Cheyenne and Lakota on the Powder River in the Yellowstone hunting grounds. After the soldiers burned down the camp, the cold forced them to retreat. Seeing his men returning to the fort with icicles hanging from their beards, Crook decided that war could wait until the summer.

CRAZY HORSE

Meanwhile, the homeless Indians found their way to Crazy Horse. After hearing their story, he led them and his own band of Oglala north, to join Sitting Bull. Other Cheyenne and Sioux fled their reservations to join the chief, too. As their numbers grew, Sitting Bull became even more determined to resist the advancing armies.

A message went out, calling all Indians west of the Missouri River to come to his camp in Wyoming. By late spring, they were fifteen thousand strong.

Sitting Bull believed they might succeed, if they fought the *wasichu* together. He rode through the huge camp, singing to give the people courage:

You tribes, what are you saying?
I have been a war chief.
All the same, I'm still living.

In mid-June he performed the Sun Dance, hoping for a vision. He danced for two days and a night, and he fell into a trance.

Then a vision did come to Sitting Bull. Swarms of bluecoats fell into the camp upside down, and a voice said, "I give these to you because they have no ears."

Sitting Bull understood his vision. The bluecoats "had no ears" because they never listened to him. They were upside down, which meant they were dead. And they were falling into Sitting Bull's camp because he and his people were going to defeat them.

Chapter 6
Little Bighorn

Sitting Bull's vision became a reality at the Battle of Little Bighorn. It was fought on June 25, 1876. The US Army officers in charge—General Alfred H. Terry, Lt. Col. George Armstrong Custer, and Brig. Gen. John Gibbon—never dreamed they could lose.

Their plan seemed foolproof. Three large forces would attack the huge Indian camp, which was spread out along the Little Bighorn River. Terry and Gibbon, with rifles, cannons, and Gatlings (early machine guns), would station themselves at the north end of the camp.

Meanwhile, Custer, along with Major Marcus Reno and Captain Frederick Benteen, would lead the Seventh Cavalry in an attack on the south end of the camp. The Indians would flee to the north, straight into Terry and Gibbon and their big guns.

Many things went wrong with the plan. For days, Custer's Crow scouts had been telling him he was outnumbered. He should wait for Terry and Gibbon, who were coming from the east with heavy ammunition. But Custer ignored them. In his opinion, there weren't enough Indians in the country to beat the Seventh Cavalry! As luck would have it, bends in the river,

rees, and hills kept him from seeing how big the
ndian camp really was, even on the day of battle.

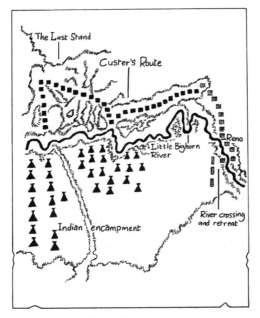

The Last Stand

Custer's Route

Little Bighorn
River

Reno

River crossing
and retreat

Indian encampment

BATTLE OF THE LITTLE BIGHORN, 1876

Custer was also overeager to fight. He wanted
all the fame and glory that would come if he
defeated the Indians. And he feared they would
escape unless he took them by surprise. So when
Custer got word that his troops had been spotted
that morning, he made some hasty decisions.

He split up the cavalry, sending Benteen and 150 men into the hills near the river, to scout for Indians.

He sent Reno and 150 men across the river, to attack the south end of the Indian camp. After promising to send them reinforcements, he and his men rode toward the north end of the camp, to attack it there.

Reno's part of the battle didn't go well. When he and his men got off their horses and started shooting, about nine hundred Indian warriors, including Sitting Bull, came at them. Reno quickly led a retreat back across the river and up a hill. Many of his men were killed on the way. The rest survived because Sitting Bull left them there. But it wasn't out of kindness.

When the chief first saw Reno and his men getting off their horses to fight, he wondered why. He knew that hand-to-hand combat put the cavalry at a disadvantage. He guessed (correctly) that Reno was expecting help from other soldiers on horseback. But if so, where were they?

Then he saw Custer and about 250 bluecoats on a distant ridge, riding toward the north end of camp. They had to be stopped, so Sitting Bull ordered his warriors away from Reno and sent them after Custer. The Indians surrounded Custer and began to shoot.

As they closed in, Custer finally understood how badly outnumbered he was. But it was much too late. The Indians killed him, and every single one of his men, in less than an hour.

LT. COL. GEORGE ARMSTRONG CUSTER

GEORGE ARMSTRONG CUSTER, BORN IN OHIO IN 1839, FOUGHT FOR THE UNION DURING THE CIVIL WAR AND BECAME THE ARMY'S YOUNGEST

GENERAL AT AGE TWENTY-THREE. HAILED AS "THE BOY GENERAL" IN THE PRESS, HE WAS KNOWN FOR GREAT DARING AND EVEN GREATER LUCK. SOMEHOW, HE HAD NEVER BEEN WOUNDED. THE INDIANS CALLED HIM **LONG HAIR** (AND SOMETIMES **YELLOW HAIR**) BECAUSE OF HIS REDDISH-BLOND CURLS.

CUSTER LED THE US ARMY'S SEVENTH CAVALRY REGIMENT AGAINST THE CHEYENNE AND THE LAKOTA MANY TIMES BETWEEN 1867 AND 1874. HE ALWAYS GOT AWAY WITHOUT A SCRATCH. HIS FAME AS AN INDIAN FIGHTER GREW, HELPED ALONG BY THE MAGAZINE ARTICLES HE WROTE ABOUT HIS DARING EXPLOITS.

IN 1876, CUSTER CONFIDED TO HIS CROW
SCOUTS THAT AFTER HE WIPED OUT THE SIOUX,
HE PLANNED TO RUN FOR PRESIDENT. BUT HIS
FAMOUS LUCK RAN OUT ON JUNE 25 THAT YEAR,
WHEN HE FOUGHT SITTING BULL, CRAZY HORSE,
AND THEIR WARRIORS AT THE BATTLE OF LITTLE
BIGHORN.

The Battle of Little Bighorn was a triumph for Sitting Bull and the nontreaty Indians. After burying and mourning their dead, they celebrated for days. Now, at last, the *wasichu* had learned their lesson. They would leave the territory so the tribes could hunt in peace. The bad times were over!

But in fact, they were about to get much worse. Custer's defeat shocked and angered the American public. The government responded by sending thousands of troops to

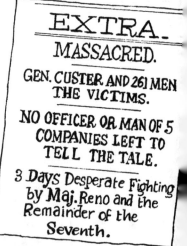

EXTRA.
MASSACRED.
GEN. CUSTER AND 261 MEN THE VICTIMS.
NO OFFICER OR MAN OF 5 COMPANIES LEFT TO TELL THE TALE.
3 Days Desperate Fighting by Maj. Reno and the Remainder of the Seventh.

the Yellowstone hunting grounds. Their mission was led by two generals who had fought for the North and burned down entire Southern cities during the Civil War. Now they did the same to the Indian villages in their path. They kept on even during the winter, forcing the nontreaty Indians to choose between starvation and surrender. By 1877, most of the Indians had moved to reservations.

The exception was Sitting Bull. He had decided that almost anything was better than giving up, even leaving the United States. So in 1877, he led about two thousand Lakota and Cheyenne across the border into Canada. There, he was told that he and his people had to follow the rules of the Grandmother (England's Queen Victoria). They had to cooperate fully with her soldiers if they wanted to stay. Sitting Bull gave his word. He intended to keep it. But even he couldn't keep trouble away.

Chapter 7
Surrender

It was against the Grandmother's rules to cross the border back into the United States. It was also against the rules to fight other Indian tribes or steal their horses. These new restrictions made it much harder for Sitting Bull's men to hunt. In Canada, they had to compete for buffalo with other tribes like the Blackfeet, Cree, and Slota. When the buffalo began to die out, food became very scarce.

Driven by hunger, people began to leave Sitting Bull's camp for the Sioux reservation in the United States. There, at least, they'd be fed. Less than four years after coming to Canada, fewer than two hundred Hunkpapa remained, and they were facing starvation.

Sitting Bull had always been able to provide food for his people. Now they were wasting away. He couldn't bear it. In July 1881, he led the last of them back to the United States, to Fort Buford in North Dakota. He was so unwilling to surrender that he gave his rifle to his young son Crow Foot, telling the boy to hand it to the authorities.

"I wish it to be remembered," he said, "that I was the last man of my tribe to surrender my rifle. This boy has given it to you, and now he wants to know how he is going to make a living."

Even after giving himself up, Sitting Bull worried army officials. They knew thousands of

Indians respected him as a great chief. If he lived among them on a reservation, he might lead an uprising. So after promising that he would soon move to the Standing Rock reservation in North Dakota, the army sent him to live at Fort Randall,

FORT RANDALL ARMY POST, 1880s

in South Dakota, instead. He, his family, and the other remaining Hunkpapa were kept there as prisoners of war for nearly two years.

Sitting Bull made many requests for release. They were ignored until a Sioux chief named Strike-the-Ree wrote to the Secretary of War. Strike-the-Ree was at the Standing Rock reservation. Sitting Bull was all the way across the

Missouri River. Yet, "his moaning cry comes to my ear," wrote the chief. "There is no one else to speak for him, so I plead his cause."

At last, in May 1883, Sitting Bull was allowed to move to Standing Rock. A rude shock awaited him there. The agent in charge, Major James McLaughlin, told him he was not a great chief, but just another Indian. He couldn't distribute food to the Hunkpapa, as a chief would. He couldn't live in a tepee, the way he had at Fort Randall. His new home would be a dark little log cabin, the same as all the others on the reservation. Then McLaughlin gave Sitting Bull a hoe and put him to work in the fields.

MAJOR JAMES
MCLAUGHLIN

In short, the agent did everything he could to make Sitting Bull feel small and powerless.

Sitting Bull never lost his temper, or his dignity. McLaughlin was a petty man—an annoyance, not a threat. When a railroad official invited Sitting Bull—not McLaughlin—to the opening ceremony for the Northern Pacific Railroad, the agent seethed

Fortunately, he never heard Sitting Bull's speech.
Given in Lakota, it went like this:

"I hate all the white people. You are thieves and
liars. You have taken away our land and made us
outcasts." The chief's interpreter, a young bluecoat,
was shocked. He quickly came up with some
friendly words in English, and the audience gave
Sitting Bull a standing ovation.

After this, Sitting Bull's fame grew. Many white people were curious about "the slayer of General Custer," as some called him. They wanted to see him in person. This annoyed McLaughlin, but impressed a showman called "Buffalo Bill" Cody.

Once a Union cavalryman and then a buffalo hunter, Cody ran a traveling show he called the Wild West. It was part circus and part rodeo, with cowboys, Indians, soldiers, and actors playing settlers. They re-created famous moments in the history of westward expansion. Crowds across the United States and Canada flocked to the show.

One of the brightest attractions was a sharpshooter named Annie Oakley. She was a petite woman with a pretty smile. Oakley could hit just about any target—the lit end of a cigarette, the thin edge of a playing card—and make it look easy.

Cody persuaded Sitting Bull to join the show in 1885. Soon, the chief and Oakley became friends. He admired her amazing skill with a rifle and named her "Little Sure Shot." He even adopted her as his daughter.

She was struck by his generosity. Most of his pay "went into the pockets of small, ragged boys," she said. "Nor could he understand how so much wealth could go brushing by, unmindful of the poor." Oakley, too, always gave money and free tickets to poor children before shows.

By the end of the season, Sitting Bull had seen enough of the white man's world. He was "sick of the houses and the noises and the multitude of men," and disliked the way money ruled their lives. "The white man knows how to make everything," he said, "but he does not know how to distribute it." He wanted to return to his family, which included his wives Seen By Her Nation and Four Robes, two daughters, and four sons.

In 1887, Buffalo Bill invited him rejoin the show when it sailed to England. The chief could meet the Grandmother herself!

Sitting Bull wouldn't go. "I am needed here," he said. "There is more talk of taking our lands." He knew that government officials once again were trying to take away part of the Great Sioux

Reservation. Their plan was to move all the Indians to half the reservation. They would sell the rest, about eleven million acres, to white settlers.

Sitting Bull had always opposed the plan. If it went through, the Lakota's shrinking world would become even smaller. By law, three-quarters of the reservation chiefs had to agree to the proposal. At first, many more than Sitting Bull were against it. But in 1889, with promises of money and acreage, and threats of reduced food rations, government agents got their way. The chiefs signed. One of the few who did not was Sitting Bull.

Later that year, life got even worse for the Lakota. Congress voted to reduce their beef rations. A severe drought caused crops to fail. Many went hungry. Others fell ill with whooping cough, influenza, and measles. Without medicine or food, people weakened and died, including two of Sitting Bull's young children. Those who lived grew angry as well as hungry. The government had cheated them again.

Then hope came—a new religion called the Ghost Dance.

Sitting Bull had always been a spiritual leader, as well as a warrior. In 1890, he listened thoughtfully when visiting Ghost Dancers promised a new and better life through their religion. He didn't believe them, but he saw nothing wrong with the dancing. It raised his people's spirits in a dark time. That was good enough.

The Ghost Dance spread across the

reservations quickly that year. Dancers prayed and had visions, wearing "ghost shirts" that supposedly protected them from bullets. Hearing this, whites feared that the Indians were really doing a war dance and planning  to rebel. It wasn't long before US military leaders decided to intervene. By December, more than six thousand soldiers had been sent to the area around Standing Rock.

Meanwhile, Major James McLaughlin was using the unrest to hurt Sitting Bull. He had already written to the government in Washington, DC. He said that the chief was "a liar and a villain" and should be arrested before he led an uprising. The only way to avoid bloodshed, claimed the agent, was to throw Sitting Bull into prison.

THE GHOST DANCE

BY THE 1880S, MOST AMERICAN INDIANS LIVED ON RESERVATIONS. THERE, THEY WERE ENCOURAGED TO FORGET THEIR CULTURE AND LIVE LIKE WHITE PEOPLE. THIS MEANT FARMING INSTEAD OF HUNTING, LIVING IN LOG HOUSES INSTEAD OF TEPEES, AND SENDING THEIR CHILDREN AWAY TO CHRISTIAN, ENGLISH-SPEAKING SCHOOLS.

MANY INDIANS MISSED THEIR OLD LIVES AND TURNED TO A NEW RELIGION CALLED THE GHOST DANCE FOR COMFORT. BASED ON THE VISION OF A PAIUTE HOLY MAN CALLED WOVOKA, THE GHOST DANCE PROMISED A WONDERFUL FUTURE FOR BELIEVERS. THEY BELIEVE THAT IF THEY DANCED, PRAYED, AND REMAINED PEACEFUL, THEY WOULD REGAIN THEIR LAND.

THE *WASICHU* WOULD DISAPPEAR FOREVER. AND
THE GHOSTS OF THEIR LOVED ONES WOULD
RETURN. SO WOULD THE BUFFALO HERDS. LIFE
WOULD BE GOOD AGAIN.

McLaughlin had also been training a group of young Hunkpapa to become policemen. Given money, extra food rations, uniforms, and weapons, they loyally followed his orders. The other Indians called them Metal Breasts because of their brass badges. When Sitting Bull ignored McLaughlin's demands to stop the Ghost Dances, the agent added more men to the force.

Sitting Bull probably didn't know that he was being blamed for encouraging "war dances." He had other worries. In November, while tending his horses on the prairie, he had heard the song of a meadowlark. As he listened, the song changed into Lakota. Its message was chilling: "One of your people will kill you."

On December 14, McLaughlin learned that Sitting Bull was about to visit Ghost Dancers at the nearby Pine Ridge reservation. He ordered a Metal Breast called Bull Head to arrest the chief the following day. "You must not let him escape," he said, "under any circumstances."

Just before dawn on December 15, forty-three Metal Breasts surrounded the chief's cabin. Bull Head and some other policemen rushed in, woke Sitting Bull, and pulled him outside before he was fully dressed. A crowd of friends and relatives had gathered and were shouting at the police to let the chief go. An Indian called Catch the Bear shot Bull Head. Before he fell, Bull Head shot back, and his bullet hit Sitting Bull in the chest.

Another Metal Breast shot Sitting Bull in the back of his head. The chief died instantly. He was fifty-nine years old.

A few months before his death, Sitting Bull wrote this song:

My father has given me this nation,
In protecting them I have a hard time.

Even when the fight seemed hopeless, Sitting Bull never stopped fighting for his people. His generosity, courage, endurance, and wisdom are admired to this day.

TIMELINE OF
SITTING BULL'S LIFE

1831	Born near Yellowstone River in South Dakota to mother, Mixed Day, and father, Returns Again
1841	First buffalo hunt
1845	Counts first coup in fight with Crow; given name Tatanka Iyotanka (Sitting Bull)
1851	Fort Laramie Treaty and first reduction of Lakota territory Marries Light Hair, who later dies in childbirth
1856	First Sun Dance
1857	Made war chief of Strong Heart Society
1863	First fights against US cavalry
1868	Made chief of Great Sioux Nation Second Fort Laramie Treaty creates Great Sioux Reservation
1872	Marries Seen By Her Nation and Four Robes
1876	Battle of Little Bighorn
1877	Moves to Canada with family and followers
1881	Surrenders at Fort Buford and is imprisoned at Fort Randall
1883	Moves to Standing Rock reservation
1885	Tours with Buffalo Bill and the Wild West
1890	Shot and killed at Standing Rock reservation

TIMELINE OF THE WORLD

Missouri Fur Company opens trading post on Missouri River Plains Indians trade animal skins for guns, sugar, and alcohol	1809
Erie Canal opens	1825
Indian Removal Act forces fifteen thousand American Indians west of the Mississippi River	1838
California Gold Rush	1848
Civil War begins Gatling gun is invented	1861
Abraham Lincoln approves building a transcontinental railroad through Indian territory	1862
Civil War ends Thirteenth Amendment abolishes slavery	1865
Nebraska becomes a state	1867
Transcontinental railroad completed	1869
First government boarding school for Indian children opens in Carlisle, Pennsylvania Little Bighorn battlefield becomes a national monument	1879
North Dakota, South Dakota, and Montana become states	1889
Dedication of "Peace Through Unity" memorial to Indians killed at Little Bighorn	2003

BIBLIOGRAPHY

Brown, Dee. **Bury My Heart at Wounded Knee: An Indian History of the American West**. New York: Holt, Rinehart & Winston, 1970.

* Davis, Kenneth C. **Don't Know Much About Sitting Bull**. New York: HarperCollins Publishers, 2003.

Dixon, Joseph K. **The Vanishing Race: The Last Great Indian Council**. Garden City, NY: Nelson Doubleday Partners & Company, 1913.

* Freedman, Russell. **Indian Chiefs**. New York: Holiday House, 1987.

LaPointe, Ernie. **Sitting Bull: His Life and Legacy**. Layton, UT: Gibbs Smith, 2009.

Ostler, Jeffrey. **The Plains Sioux and US Colonialism from Lewis and Clark to Wounded Knee**. New York: Cambridge University Press, 2004.

* Spinner, Stephanie. **Who Was Annie Oakley?** New York: Grosset & Dunlap, 2002.

* Stanley, George Edward. **Sitting Bull, Great Sioux Hero**. New York: Sterling Publishing, 2010.

Stirling, M. W. **Three Pictographic Autobiographies of Sitting Bull**. Washington, DC: Smithsonian Miscellaneous Collections, 1938.

Utley, Robert M. **The Lance and the Shield: The Life and Times of Sitting Bull**. New York: Henry Holt & Company, 1993.

Vestal, Stanley. **Sitting Bull: Champion of the Sioux**. Norman, OK: University of Oklahoma Press, 1957.

Yenne, Bill. **Sitting Bull**. Yardley, PA: Westholme Publishing, 2008.

* Books for young readers

WEBSITES

accessgenealogy.com

aimovement.org

ANB.org

nmai.si.edu

pbs.org/weta/thewest/program

sittingbull.org

sittingbullfamilyfoundation.org